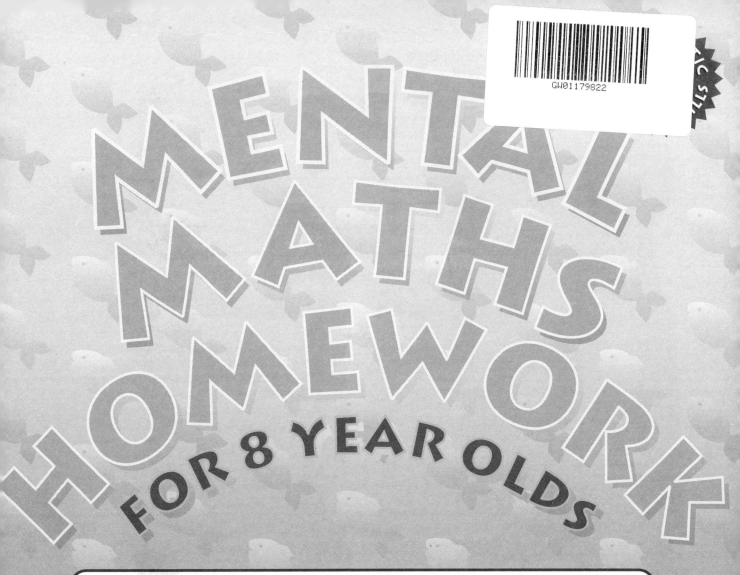

MENTAL MATHS HOMEWORK FOR 8 YEAR OLDS

SERIES EDITOR
Lin Taylor
The IMPACT Project, University of North London Enterprises Ltd

AUTHORS
Kath Morgan and Ceri Morgan

EDITOR
Joel Lane

ASSISTANT EDITOR
David Sandford

SERIES DESIGNER
Anna Oliwa

DESIGNER
Paul Roberts

ILLUSTRATIONS
Fred Pipes

COVER ARTWORK
James Alexander/David Oliver
Berkeley Studios

Text © 2000 Ceri Morgan and Kath Morgan
© 2000 Scholastic Ltd

Designed using Adobe Pagemaker
Published by Scholastic Ltd, Villiers House, Clarendon Avenue, Leamington Spa, Warwickshire CV32 5PR

1 2 3 4 5 6 7 8 9 0   0 1 2 3 4 5 6 7 8 9

British Library Cataloguing-in-Publication Data
A catalogue record for this book is available from the British Library.

ISBN 0-439-01704-1

The right of Kath Morgan and Ceri Morgan to be identified as the authors of this work has been asserted by them in accordance with the Copyright, Designs and Patents Act 1988.

All rights reserved. This book is sold subject to the condition that it shall not, by way of trade or otherwise, be lent, hired out or otherwise circulated without the publisher's prior consent in any form of binding or cover other than that in which it is published and without a similar condition, including this condition, being imposed upon the subsequent purchaser.

No part of this publication may be reproduced, stored in a retrieval system, or transmitted, in any form or by any means, electronic, mechanical, photocopying, recording or otherwise, without the prior permission of the publisher. This book remains copyright, although permission is granted to copy pages 9–48 for classroom distribution and use only in the school which has purchased the book and in accordance with the CLA licensing agreement. Photocopying permission is given only for purchasers and not for borrowers of books from any lending service.

INTRODUCTION 3
TEACHERS' NOTES 5

COUNTING AND ORDERING

COUNTDOWN	9	counting back in steps
CAR START	10	counting on in 10s from large numbers
5S CHAINS	11	counting on in steps of 5
DICE DIGITS	12	ordering three-digit numbers
SHOPPING LIST	13	ordering amounts of money
SCOREBOARD	14	making numbers using H, T and U
STRING IT ALONG	15	ordering simple fractions
ORDER THE DRINKS	16	ordering measures of capacity

ADDITION AND SUBTRACTION

MAKE 20	17	finding complements of 20
CROSS IT OUT	18	making target numbers by addition
MAKE IT	19	making sentences with given numbers
CHAIN REACTION	20	carrying out + and – instructions
A NUMBER CLOUD	21	making totals from a set of numbers
SUBTRACTION SAM	22	identifying a subtraction function
CALENDAR TIME	23	adding near-multiples of 10
TAKE IT UP	24	recalling addition bonds of 20
TOP SCORER	25	making target numbers by addition
GOAL SCORERS	26	
MAKING MESSY NUMBERS	27	adding chains of numbers
UP AND DOWN DICE	28	adding and subtracting multiples of 10
TELEPHONE KEYPAD	29	making target totals with four numbers
CALCULATOR KEYPAD	30	making target totals with six numbers
MORE KEYPADS	31	
CROSS AND COUNT	32	keeping a running total of numbers

MULTIPLICATION AND DIVISION

HALVE AND HALVE AGAIN	33	using repeated halving to ÷4
LINE UP	34	recalling 5 times table facts
DOG FOOD	35	identifying multiples of 3, 4 and 5
PICKLES THE GREEDY CAT	36	dividing by 4 with remainders
BECKY'S BUGS	37	practising the 3 times table
FOUR THROWS	38	identifying multiples of 4
DIVIDE AND RULE	39	identifying multiples of numbers 1 to 6
MORE TRACKS	40	
WINNING GOAL	41	recalling × and ÷ facts
MONSTER DIGITS	42	using repeated tripling to ×81

MULTISTEP AND MIXED OPERATIONS

ROLL AND ROLL AGAIN	43	multiplying by 10 and subtracting
TARGET 75	44	making a target total by +, – and ×
GOING UNDERGROUND	45	combining + and × calculations
PRINTING PROBLEMS	46	solving a problem using × and place value
CHAIN LINKS	47	carrying out +, – and × instructions

LETTER TO HELPER 48

ABOUT HOMEWORK

Homework can be a very useful opportunity to practise and develop children's understanding of the work done in school. Games and maths challenges can be very good activities to share with someone at home, especially to develop mental maths strategies and maths language skills. Research* indicates that parental involvement is a major factor in children's educational success. Most parents want to help their children with their school work, but often do not know how and 'traditional' homework does not involve parents. Shared homework activities, such as can be found in Mental Maths Homework, are designed to be completed with a parent or helper, such as a sibling, neighbour or other adult who can work with the child. Working one-to-one with an adult in the home environment really has a powerful effect. The National Numeracy Strategy strongly supports this type of homework, which is in line with a variety of government guidelines on the role of parents and making home links.

ABOUT MENTAL MATHS AT HOME

Mental Maths Homework is particularly concerned to develop children's mental mathematics. In order to become competent at mental calculation, children need to talk about mathematics and try out different strategies, as well as to practise number facts and skills. Children explaining their mathematics to a parent or helper can help to clarify and develop their understanding of the mathematics. This type of homework, developed by The IMPACT Project, is a joint activity: the helper and child working together.

ABOUT MENTAL MATHS HOMEWORK

This series comprises of six books, one for each age group from 6–11 years (Year 1/P2–Year 6/P7). Each book contains 36 photocopiable activities – enough for one to be sent home each week throughout the school year, if you wish. The activities concentrate on the number system and developing children's calculation strategies and are designed to fit into your planning, whatever scheme you are using. Since these books are designed to support the same aims of developing mental maths strategies and vocabulary, they make an ideal follow-on to the class work outlined in Scholastic's other Mental Maths series. The objectives for each activity are based on those in the National Numeracy Strategy Framework for Teaching Mathematics and the content is appropriate for teachers following other UK curriculum documents.

USING THE ACTIVITIES IN SCHOOL

Although the books are designed for a particular age group they should be used flexibly so that the right level of activity is set for a child or class. All the activities are photocopiable: most are one page, some are two, or require an extra resource page (to be found at the back of the book) for certain games or number card activities. The activities for older children will generally take longer than those for younger children.

BEFORE

It is essential that each activity is introduced to the class before it is sent home with them. This fulfils several crucial functions. It enables the child to explain the activity to the parent or carer; ensuring the child understands the task. It also familiarises the child with the activity; developing motivation and making the activity more accessible. This initial introduction to the activity can be done as part of a regular maths lesson, at the end of the day, or whenever fits in with your class's routine.

AFTER

It is also important that the child brings something back to school from the activity at home. This will not necessarily be substantial, or even anything written, since the activities aim to develop mental mathematics. It is equally important that what the child brings in from home is genuinely valued by you. It is unlikely that parents will be encouraged to share activities with their children if they do not feel that their role is valued either. Each activity indicates what should be brought back to school, and the teachers' notes (on pages 5–8) offer guidance on introducing and working with or reviewing the outcome of each activity.

HELPERS

All the activities have a note to the helper explaining the purpose of the activity and how to help the child, often emphasizing useful vocabulary. The helpers' notes also give indications of how to adapt the activity at home, and what to do if the child gets stuck. Many of the activities are games or fun activities which it is hoped that the parent and child will enjoy doing together and will do again, even when not set for homework, thus increasing the educational benefit. It is particularly beneficial for a game to be played a number of times.

OTHER WAYS TO USE THE ACTIVITIES

The activities offered in Mental Maths Homework are very flexible and will be used in different ways in

different schools. As well as being used for shared homework, they could form the basis of a display or a school challenge, or be used as activities for a maths club. Or, they could be used independently of the school situation by parents who wish to provide stimulating and appropriate educational activities for their children.

USING THE ACTIVITIES AT HOME
If you are a parent using these activities outside of school:
- Choose an activity you both think looks interesting and get going straight away with your child. Make the work *joint:* the helper and the child working out what has to be done *together*.
- Read the instructions to your child and ask him or her to explain what has to be done. It is very effective for the child to do the explaining.

USING HOMEWORK DIARIES
Developing a dialogue between teacher and parent is an important part of shared homework. By working with the child at home, the parent becomes more familiar with the mathematics of the classroom. The teacher also needs to hear from the parent about how the child is faring with the activities. Diaries provide a very good mechanism for this. The helpers and/or the children can comment on the activities (which will give you important feedback) and individual targets can be put into the diary. The diaries can act, therefore, as an important channel of communication. (See below for details about finding out more information about diaries.)

ABOUT THIS BOOK
In *Mental Maths Homework for 8 year olds*, the primary emphasis is on developing and improving skills in using number operations to solve problems. Many of these problems are based on addition, subtraction and, especially, simple multiplication operations. There is an increasing frequency of examples of problems which have more than one possible solution, or require the child to use a strategy to find an answer. This reflects the requirement within the Numeracy Framework to develop a range of mental strategies and skills.

Many of the activities also contain a prompt to discuss or investigate extensions to the actual problem posed. This may be by using the same context with different numbers, or by asking the children to make up similar problems of their own. An important element of work at this level is the ability to explain whatever strategy has been used, and it is important that the children are given this opportunity at some point in their homework.

* Bastiani, J. & Wolfendale, S. (1996) *Home-School Work: Review, Reflection and Development* David Fulton Publishers.

THE IMPACT PROJECT
The activities in *Mental Maths Homework* have all been devised by members of The IMPACT Project, based at the University of North London. The project, a pioneer of shared homework with a wealth of experience, is involved in a variety of initiatives concerning parental involvement and homework. It also supports schools in setting up a school framework for shared homework. If you would like help with developing shared homework, planning a whole-school framework for homework or developing mental mathematics at home and at school, maybe through INSET with experienced providers, contact The IMPACT Project. Information about other activities undertaken by the project and about other IMPACT books and resources, such as the IMPACT diaries, is also available from The IMPACT Project.

The IMPACT Project
University of North London
School of Education
166–220 Holloway Road
London
N7 8DB

tel. no. 020 7753 7052

fax. no. 020 7753 5420

e-mail: impact-enquiries@unl.ac.uk
    impact-orders@unl.ac.uk

web: http://www.unl.ac.uk/impact

COUNTING & ORDERING

COUNTDOWN
OBJECTIVES: To use counting as a strategy for solving problems. To understand properties of numbers.
BEFORE: Model this activity with the children. Play the dice game and ask them to count back using a small number such as 2.
AFTER: Play the game with the children and ask one of them to tell the others what he or she is doing. Play with larger numbers.

CAR START
OBJECTIVES: To develop an understanding of numbers. To explore their properties.
BEFORE: Discuss the collection of car numbers, using examples you have collected yourself. Ask how many tens there are in each of your examples (for instance, 462 has 6 tens). Model counting in tens.
AFTER: Discuss any problematic numbers (for example, moving from 95 to 105). Collect examples of counting back in tens.

5S CHAINS
OBJECTIVES: To develop an understanding of numbers. To explore counting in 5s.
BEFORE: Invite a child to help you construct a chain of numbers on the board. Start with a multiple of 5 and count on in 5s, writing the numbers as the chain is built up. Repeat, starting with a non-multiple of 5.
AFTER: Compare chains and see whether there are any discrepancies. Pair the children and ask them to read their chains to each other.

DICE DIGITS
OBJECTIVES: To sort and organize data. To investigate number properties and place value.
BEFORE: Ask the children to provide three random single-digit numbers. Write these on the board and ask the children to suggest any numbers that use all three digits. Collect different 3-digit numbers and suggest ways in which this data could be organized.
AFTER: Collect suggestions. Organize them in order, largest first. Ask the children to read out the numbers.

SHOPPING LIST
OBJECTIVES: To solve problems using money. To develop an understanding of decimals.
BEFORE: Discuss the correct format for writing amounts of money. Look at some till receipts or write amounts on the board; make sure the children are familiar with the notation. Discuss how they might choose to order these amounts.
AFTER: Ask the children to order longer shopping lists, or to read out their own three-item lists and check them for accuracy.

SCOREBOARD
OBJECTIVES: To use mental strategies in various contexts. To develop an understanding of place value.
BEFORE: Model the activity using different numbers. Discuss the idea of using a strategy to make a particular target score. Check that the children understand terms such as maximum and minimum.
AFTER: Ask some children for answers. Check these for accuracy; then ask the children to explain how they worked out where to place their counters.

STRING IT ALONG
OBJECTIVES: To develop an understanding of fractions. To place fractions in order.
BEFORE: Draw a line on the board and mark ½, ¼ and ¾ on it. Cut up shapes and objects to show these fractions. Erase the line, then ask children to mark ½ or ¼ on a blank line.
AFTER: Place a string in the classroom and invite children to show where they placed their labels. Discuss any incorrect placings.

ORDER THE DRINKS
OBJECTIVES: To order containers by estimating their capacity. To order numbers in the context of measure.
BEFORE: Show a few containers, with capacity (in metric units) on covered labels. Ask children to suggest which one holds least, then order them from smallest to largest. Uncover the labels and ask children to read out the capacity figures. List them on the board and ask: *Were we right? Why/Why not?* Discuss units if necessary.
AFTER: Discuss some of the children's lists. These could be displayed with a list of several unordered amounts and the question: *Can you order these amounts from least to most?*

ADDITION & SUBTRACTION

MAKE 20
OBJECTIVE: To use known number facts to solve problems involving number bonds to 20 (and to derive related addition facts).
BEFORE: Ask the children for two numbers that make 10. Collect suggestions on the board and count them. Ask for one or two pairs that make 20, then invite guesses as to how many pairs there might be.
AFTER: Collect answers to make a full list of the number bonds to 20. Ask how these might be ordered to check that none are missing.

CROSS IT OUT
OBJECTIVES: To add single-digit and 2-digit numbers. To develop a understanding of the properties of numbers.

BEFORE: Write some 2-digit numbers on the board. Ask for numbers from 1–6 that could be added to these. Add the suggestions to the 2-digit numbers, pairing them up to encourage specific strategies (for example, pair 29 with 1 to make a multiple of 10). Model the homework activity.
AFTER: Collect the children's answers and write them on the board. Discuss them, looking first at how the children added the tens.

MAKE IT
OBJECTIVE: To see connections between addition and subtraction.
BEFORE: Model the activity using other 'trios' of numbers. Ask the children to make addition and subtraction sentences. Encourage them to write these on the board and read them out.
AFTER: Discuss the children's sentences. Ask whether 'sets' of linked sentences can be formed (for any trio, there are two additions and two subtractions). Emphasise the link between addition and subtraction.

CHAIN REACTION
OBJECTIVE: To practise mental addition and subtraction of multiples of 10.
BEFORE: Ask the children to add or subtract first 10, then multiples of 10, to or from a given multiple of 10. Ask how they worked them out; discuss their methods.
AFTER: Discuss the children's chains. *Which ones were easy to work out? Which were more difficult? Why?* Children could make up their own chains for others to complete, perhaps providing the last 'link'.

A NUMBER CLOUD
OBJECTIVE: To add two 2-digit numbers (without crossing through tens) mentally.
BEFORE: Model the activity with a few numbers. Ask children to explain how the numbers can be added mentally. Reinforce efficient strategies, recording the steps on the board.
AFTER: Discuss the children's answers. Encourage children to explain how they worked them out. If several methods were used, give an opportunity for each method to be explained. Emphasize more efficient ways. Ask how you can check that all possible additions have been done.

SUBTRACTION SAM
OBJECTIVES: To subtract small numbers from 2-digit numbers. To identify subtraction patterns.
BEFORE: Ask the children to subtract 3 from some 2-digit numbers. Discuss how small numbers can be subtracted. Although counting back can be used, try to identify other strategies, particularly the use of known subtraction facts for numbers under 10.
AFTER: Discuss the answers for Sam, and the pattern. Display the children's subtraction machines, with a challenge beside each one: *What numbers would this machine make if we put in 100 or 1000?*

CALENDAR TIME
OBJECTIVES: To add two 2-digit numbers (without crossing through tens) mentally. To know the months of the year and the number of days in each month.
BEFORE: Use a current calendar to revise the order of the months. Ask: *Does anyone know how many days are in January? What about February? How many days are there in January and February together?* Discuss how to calculate this. Explain the activity.
AFTER: Discuss how many additions the children have done. List them on the board. Discuss how they were worked out; reinforce effective strategies. *How many different answers did we get?*

TAKE IT UP
OBJECTIVE: To gain practice with addition and subtraction bonds to 20.
BEFORE: Model the activity, but only using bonds to 10 (the children should know these facts already).
AFTER: Discuss the children's additions to 20. *Have we found them all? How can we tell?* Discuss ways of working out or remembering the number pairs. List them in order, next to those for 10; ask the children what they notice. A set of other lists brought in could be displayed.

TOP SCORER
OBJECTIVE: To use mental calculation to solve problems. To add a string of numbers.
BEFORE: Ask a child to write any number from 10–20 on the board. Ask the class to say any two numbers that add to make this number. Make a list of the number bonds. Repeat, asking for three numbers that add to make the original number. Model the activity.
AFTER: Discuss the children's solutions. Check these for accuracy. Ask whether there are any strategies which can help you find two numbers with an odd or even total. Discuss any solutions found to the problems on the 'Goal scorers' sheet.

MAKING MESSY NUMBERS
OBJECTIVE: To gain practice with multiple additions.
BEFORE: Discuss the term 'messy numbers', meaning any numbers that are not multiples of 10 or 5. Ask the children to choose any eight different numbers and add them together. Make a list of their totals on the board. Repeat, asking them to make a target number (such as 10); they may subtract as well as add.
AFTER: Collect the strings the children have suggested. Choose some examples and 'pair' the numbers in ways that encourage a systematic method. For example, rewrite a string with number bonds to 10 paired. Discuss how this makes long addition 'easier'.

UP AND DOWN DICE
OBJECTIVES: To add and subtract multiples of 10. To develop an understanding of the properties of numbers.

BEFORE: Discuss the phrase 'any multiple of 10 between 100 and 200'; agree on which numbers are included. Model the game with 100 as your target number. Suggest a way to record the results.
AFTER: Ask each child to explain how he or she made a target number, while the other children note how many dice throws were required. Make a list of the numbers made with fewer than five throws.

TELEPHONE KEYPAD
OBJECTIVES: To explore properties of numbers. To use known addition facts to solve open-ended problems.
BEFORE: Draw a keypad on the board. Ask the children to choose any four numbers. Write them on the board and add them, suggesting strategies if possible (for example, pairing 2 + 8 to make 10).
AFTER: Collect the children's totals. Compare any totals made using similar numbers (do 18 and 28 show similar patterns?). Make a list of any totals that were not made; try to make one of them.

CALCULATOR KEYPAD
OBJECTIVE: To use mental calculation to solve problems involving addition of a string of numbers.
BEFORE: Draw a keypad on the board. Invite the children to choose any number. Draw a faint line through the other numbers in that row and column (so that all the digits are still visible). Make an addition using all these numbers, discussing ways to do this; draw attention to the use of number bonds to 10.
AFTER: Ask the children for their number strings and totals. Check them for accuracy. Write the totals in order. Discuss any totals that have not been made. Try with other grids. Go through any work done using the 'More keypads' sheet, checking that the children have correctly identified diagonal number lines.

CROSS AND COUNT
OBJECTIVE: To use mental calculation to solve problems involving addition of a string of numbers.
BEFORE: Draw a 4 × 4 number grid on the board and ask a child to choose a number. Write the number on the board, then draw a faint line through the rest of that row. Write down these numbers, then add them. Repeat with the column, then add the two totals.
AFTER: Ask the children for their number strings and totals. Check them for accuracy. Ask the children to suggest new grid arrangements. Repeat the activity with larger numbers.

MULTIPLICATION & DIVISION

HALVE AND HALVE AGAIN
OBJECTIVE: To halve, then halve again, multiples of 4.
BEFORE: Practise halving some even whole numbers. Go on to halving and halving again. Discuss how the children work out the answers. Do they 'just know' some halves, or do they have a method for finding them?
AFTER: Ask some children to show others which answers they think were wrong. Display a 'halve and halve again' machine, showing 'in' numbers and asking children to find the 'out' numbers, or showing 'out' numbers and asking children to work out what the 'in' numbers were.

LINE UP
OBJECTIVE: To practise multiplying by 5.
BEFORE: Model the activity with playing cards. Ask the children how they can find the answers. Do they 'just know' some 'fives'? How could they calculate others? Encourage strategies such as multiplying by 10 and then halving.
AFTER: Did the children enjoy the game? They could play it in pairs, either using cards to generate the numbers or choosing their own numbers.

DOG FOOD
OBJECTIVES: To develop understanding of multiplication tables. To use mental calculation strategies to help solve problems.
BEFORE: Revise the 3, 4 and 5 times tables. Draw attention to common multiples. Model the activity using multiples of 2.
AFTER: Discuss the children's work. Invite them to say which 'bone numbers' are multiples of more than one 'dog number', and then to investigate which are multiples of other numbers. Make a list of numbers which are in more than two multiplication tables.

PICKLES THE GREEDY CAT
OBJECTIVES: To use mental calculations to solve word problems. To practise multiplication and division.
BEFORE: Revise the multiplication pattern for 4. Ask questions such as: *What is 3 × 4 add 1?* Invite the children to think about multiples of 4 and remainders. Model the activity, making a clear distinction between the bowls that contain multiples of 4 and those that do not.
AFTER: Ask the children for their answers; check these for accuracy. Repeat the activity with other multiplication tables.

BECKY'S BUGS
OBJECTIVE: To use repeated addition to develop an understanding of the patterns in the 3 and 4 times tables.
BEFORE: Draw a 'spider' on the board. Count the number of 'legs' together and start a pattern using the 3 times table. Check that the children know to write one number on each leg.
AFTER: Ask some children to say their number patterns. Discuss any errors. Repeat the activity with other multiplication tables (including the 2, 5 and 10 times tables as revision).

TEACHERS' NOTES

FOUR THROWS
OBJECTIVES: To practise rapid recall of multiples of 4. To solve problems by simple reasoning about numbers.
BEFORE: Demonstrate the activity. Discuss possible strategies for making a multiple of 4 when you cannot do it by adding or subtracting.
AFTER: Repeat the activity, looking for multiples of 3. Ask the children to keep a tally of how often different multiples of 3 are made.

DIVIDE AND RULE
OBJECTIVES: To develop rapid recall of multiplication and division facts.
BEFORE: Draw a track (as on page 40) on the board, with a number in each section. Use numbers that have more than one factor. Ask the children to choose a number from 1–6. Model the activity using this number. Repeat with a different number.
AFTER: Ask a child to read out his or her results. Write them on the board and go through them together. Invite the children to invent a track that will be easier to get through. Discuss the outcomes of any games played using the 'More tracks' sheet.

WINNING GOAL
OBJECTIVES: To understand multiplication and division and use them to solve problems. To develop rapid recall of multiplication facts.
BEFORE: This activity must be played in school before it is sent home. Let the children choose a 'goal' number whose times table is familiar to them. Discuss why they cannot choose 1 as their 'goal' number.
AFTER: Ask the children to play again. See how many times each child wins. Collect the scores. Discuss which 'goal' numbers are more likely to lead to a win.

MONSTER DIGITS
OBJECTIVES: To use mental calculations to solve simple word problems. To understand multiplication as repeated addition.
BEFORE: Discuss the idea of aliens with multiple limbs. Draw one on the board. Count out loud the various attributes. Write the numbers around the picture. Talk about aliens based on multiples of 3, 4 and 5.
AFTER: Display some of the children's drawings and write the numbers next to them. Discuss how the totals were found. Consider a 'hybrid' alien with two arms, three hands, four fingers and so on.

MULTISTEP & MIXED OPERATIONS

ROLL AND ROLL AGAIN
OBJECTIVES: To multiply numbers by 10. To find the difference between two multiples of 10.
BEFORE: Revise multiplying by 10 by giving two multiples of 10 and asking how the difference could be found. (Discuss the word 'difference' if necessary.) One possible strategy is counting on in 10s.
AFTER: Discuss the children's work. Ask them to explain how they worked out the answers. *Were some easier than others? Were some more difficult? Why?*

TARGET 75
OBJECTIVES: To reason about numbers. To use addition, subtraction and multiplication to solve problems.
BEFORE: Model the activity, letting the children choose which operations to use. Let them practise it to make sure they are clear about the rules.
AFTER: Repeat the activity with a group. Try rolling two dice and finding out which numbers can be made with a variety of operations in any order. Make a list of possible answers for each pair of numbers.

GOING UNDERGROUND
OBJECTIVE: To solve problems involving mental addition and subtraction of a string of numbers.
BEFORE: Ask a child to suggest a number from 1–10 and write it on the board. Ask another child to suggest an operation (addition or subtraction) and another number. Make a drawing with arrows to show the move from the original number via the operation to the tunnel.
AFTER: Collect the children's work. Choose an example, read it out and check it. Invite some children to talk the class through particular routes.

PRINTING PROBLEMS
OBJECTIVES: To use counting to support reasoning about numbers. To solve a problem by applying number facts.
BEFORE: Discuss the activity, using a small folded paper booklet with eight pages as an example. Ask how many page numbers in this booklet would be affected if the 7 did not work. Extend this to discussing how many numbers to 100 have a 7 in them.
AFTER: Invite the children to explain their answers. Ask them to write a list of which numbers from 1–100 have a 7 in them, and to explain (orally) which numbers from 1–1000 have a 7 in them.

CHAIN LINKS
OBJECTIVES: To use mental strategies and calculation skills to solve problems. To explore the properties of numbers.
BEFORE: Demonstrate how to make a 'chain' using one operation (invite the children to suggest which one). When they have a clear idea of how the chain is made, ask them to suggest different operations and to make a short chain of their own.
AFTER: Ask one child to explain his or her chain and draw it on the board. Check it for accuracy. Invite the children to swap chains with a partner for checking.

NAME _____ DATE _____

COUNTDOWN

YOU WILL NEED: A helper, a dice, pencil and paper.

YOU ARE GOING TO: play a counting backwards game.
❑ Decide who is going to start.
❑ If you are starting, choose a number between 20 and 30. Next, your helper rolls the dice. This is going to be the step number.
❑ Starting with your chosen number, count back in steps of the dice number. Write each number down as you count. So if your chosen number was 27 and the dice number was 5, you would write: 27, 22, 17...
❑ Keep going until you reach a number **less than 10**. If the number you reach is 9, 8 or 7, you score 1 point. If you reach 6, 5 or 4, you score 2 points.

❑ Now it is your helper's turn to start. Carry on playing until you have had four turns each. Which of you has more points?
❑ Take some of the lists of numbers back to school.

BET YOU CAN'T
Play again, throwing a coin and counting back in steps of 6 (heads) or 7 (tails).

0 1 2 3 4 5 6 7 8 9 10 11 12 13 14 15 16 17 18 19 20 21 22 23 24 25 26 27 28 29 30

DEAR HELPER
THE POINT OF THIS ACTIVITY: is to help your child count backwards and develop his or her sense of numbers. He or she can use the number line on this page to count back. This game will also support your child's subtraction skills.
  Encourage your child to say the numbers clearly while counting backwards, and to check his or her lists of numbers.

YOU MIGHT LIKE TO: start with bigger numbers. You could also choose bigger numbers for step numbers.

IF YOU GET STUCK: use smaller numbers to start with and count back in 1s, 2s or 3s. (You can do this by covering the 4, 5 and 6 on the dice with stickers saying 1, 2 and 3).

Please sign: . . . .

NAME   **DATE**

CAR START

YOU WILL NEED: A helper, pencil and paper, four car numbers that you have found and written down. (If you can't find any car numbers, just write down four numbers smaller than 1000.)

YOU ARE GOING TO: count up in steps of 10.
❏ Read out your four numbers to your helper.
❏ Take turns to choose one of the car numbers and count on from it in 10s – as far as you can! Write down each number that you count.

❏ Take your longest list of numbers back to school.

BET YOU CAN'T:
❏ Count on from each number in 100s – and keep going!
❏ Count back in 10s from each number.

DEAR HELPER

THE POINT OF THIS ACTIVITY: is to help your child develop his or her understanding of numbers. It should also help him or her with reading and speaking numbers. The numerical part of a number plate may be either a 2-figure or a 3-figure number. Make sure your child does not confuse 0 (zero) with the letter O.

Encourage your child to write down the numbers as they are spoken, in order to make the link between spoken and written numbers. Stop the counting in 10s at the next thousand, if not before.

YOU MIGHT LIKE TO: make up number plates which immediately require your child to count through a hundred (as in 296) or a thousand (as in 998).

IF YOU GET STUCK:
● Your child may need some help to get started. Say aloud (for example) '236, 246, 256' – then see whether your child can carry on. If he or she finds that difficult, choose a 2-digit number to count on from (for example, '21, 31, 41').
● If your child gets stuck going through the next hundred, leave it there and start again with a new number (perhaps one less than 100).

Please sign: . . . .

5S CHAINS

YOU WILL NEED: A helper, pencil and paper.

YOU ARE GOING TO: make some '5s chains' by counting in steps of 5.

❏ Here is your first chain. Take turns with your helper to add on 5. What do you notice?

❏ Now try this one:

❏ Try this one. Can you fill in all the numbers on your own?

❏ Now use the blank chains below to write your own '5s chains'. You can use any starting numbers you like.

❏ Take all the chains you have done back to school.

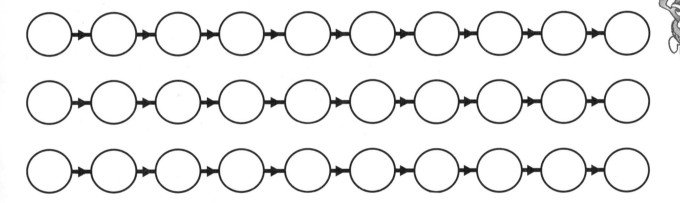

BET YOU CAN'T
❏ Make a 5s chain with 54 in the middle of it.
❏ Make a 5s chain with 46 near the end.

DEAR HELPER
THE POINT OF THIS ACTIVITY: is to help your child count in fives and see the patterns which occur. This will help your child to develop his or her addition skills.

YOU MIGHT LIKE TO: make up a starting number and ask your child to find the next two numbers.

IF YOU GET STUCK: help your child to notice that when we keep on adding 5, we get the same two 'units' digits alternating. Saying the numbers aloud can help to make this clear.

Please sign: . . . .

DICE DIGITS

YOU WILL NEED: A helper, a dice, pencil and paper.

YOU ARE GOING TO: put different numbers in order.
- ❑ Roll the dice three times and write down the digits.
- ❑ With your helper, see how many **different** 3-digit numbers you can make with the digits. Write them all down.
- ❑ Now try to put the 3-digit numbers in order, with the largest first.
- ❑ Roll the dice another three times and try again.

- ❑ Take your lists of numbers back to school.

BET YOU CAN'T
Roll three more digits, then write down only the largest and smallest possible numbers you can make with them.

DEAR HELPER

THE POINT OF THIS ACTIVITY: is to help your child put 3-digit numbers in order. It will help if you and your child say the numbers before you order them together.

YOU MIGHT LIKE TO: use the playing cards Ace to 9 and pick three cards for digits, instead of using a dice.

IF YOU GET STUCK: encourage your child to find all the possible numbers that can be made with three digits (there are six if all the digits are different). If he or she runs out of ideas, stress the hundreds number: *Six hundred and twenty-three is more than **two** hundred and sixty-three.* Then stress the tens number: *Two hundred and **sixty**-three is more than two hundred and **thirty**-six.*

Please sign: . . . .

NAME   DATE

SHOPPING LIST

YOU WILL NEED: A helper, a supermarket till receipt, pencil and paper.

YOU ARE GOING TO: put different amounts of money in order.
- ❏ Find three items on the receipt with different prices, each item less than £5.
- ❏ Write down these three items and their prices.
- ❏ Now write them in order of price, with the largest amount first.

- ❏ Bring your ordered numbers back to school.

BET YOU CAN'T
Find the most expensive item priced below £5.

DEAR HELPER
THE POINT OF THIS ACTIVITY: is to help your child order decimal numbers in the context of money. Encourage your child to read out the amounts.

IF YOU GET STUCK:
- Look at amounts less than £1 to start with.
- Order two amounts if your child finds three difficult.

YOU MIGHT LIKE TO: try finding and ordering four different prices.

Please sign: . . . .

SCOREBOARD

YOU WILL NEED: A helper, six counters or buttons, the scoreboard on this page, pencil and paper.

YOU ARE GOING TO: make numbers using hundreds, tens and ones.
❏ Place the six counters anywhere on the scoreboard shown here.
❏ What score did you get? Explain to your helper how you got that score.
❏ Now make and explain some different scores.
❏ Bring your counters and a list of your scores back to school. Be ready to show how you made them.

YOU MIGHT LIKE TO TRY
Making these numbers (you must use all six counters each time):
❏ the highest number possible
❏ the lowest number possible
❏ a number between 300 and 350
❏ a number between 200 and 230
❏ an even number between 20 and 30.
❏ Talk about these with your partner.

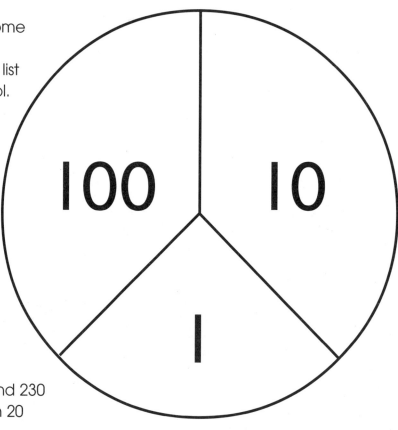

DEAR HELPER

THE POINT OF THIS ACTIVITY: is to help your child understand our number system (units, tens, hundreds and so on). Encourage your child to explain how each score was made.
   The further challenges require your child to apply some of his or her mathematical skills.

YOU MIGHT LIKE TO: set each other some different challenges. For example: *How many numbers can you make between 100 and 200?*

IF YOU GET STUCK: leave the further challenges and just continue to make various scores. Then ask your child to order the set of numbers he or she has made.

Please sign: . . . .

| NAME | DATE |

STRING IT ALONG

YOU WILL NEED: A helper, a piece of string (or ribbon) about half a metre long, scissors, paper and pencil (or marker pen), the labels on this page – and some space on the floor.

YOU ARE GOING TO: put some fractions in order.

❑ Lay out the string in a straight line on the floor.

❑ Decide how you can find halfway along it. Make a mark on the string to show where this is.

❑ Now find halfway between one end and the mark. Put another mark here. Find halfway between the other end and the centre mark. Put a mark there.

❑ Cut out the labels on this page. Put 0 at one end of the string and 1 at the other end. Then place ¼, ½ and ¾ where you think they should go.

❑ Bring your marked string and labels back into school. Be ready to show where on the string the labels should go.

BET YOU CAN'T
Shuffle the labels, then put them one by one in the right places on the string.

DEAR HELPER

THE POINT OF THIS ACTIVITY: is to help your child find and order some common fractions.

YOU MIGHT LIKE TO:
● Take the labels off the string and ask your child to point to where the ¾ label should go, where ¼ should go and so on.

● Point to a place on the string and ask: *Which label should go in this place?*

IF YOU GET STUCK: help your child place 0 and 1. Ask *Where should ½ go?* and then *Which is smaller, ¼ or ¾?*

Please sign: . . . .

ORDER THE DRINKS

YOU WILL NEED: A helper, four or five empty drinks cans or bottles of different sizes, pencil and paper.

YOU ARE GOING TO: rearrange some containers so that they are in order of how much they hold.

❏ Without looking at the labels, try to put your drinks containers in order. Start with the one you think holds least.

❏ Ask your helper whether he or she agrees with your order.

❏ Now find out how much drink each can or bottle holds. This is usually shown on the label.

❏ Were you right? If not, put the containers in the right order.

❏ Write down the amounts you have put in order. Bring this list into school.

BET YOU CAN'T
Think of a container that would hold more more than any of the ones you've put in order. What sort of container might it be?

DEAR HELPER

THE POINT OF THIS ACTIVITY: is to help your child order numbers. It will also help him or her to start learning about capacity.

Use any cans or bottles which show their capacity in millilitres (ml). Make sure that the containers used are empty, have been rinsed out and have no jagged edges. Encourage your child to read out the amounts shown on the containers after he or she has initially ordered them.

YOU MIGHT LIKE TO: look at some other containers you have in the kitchen. How much do they hold?

IF YOU GET STUCK:
● Order just two cans or bottles to start with.
● Help your child to read out the amounts if he or she finds this difficult.
● Your child could also try writing down the amounts, as seeing and hearing numbers at the same time can help with understanding them.

Please sign: . . . .

NAME												DATE

MAKE 20

YOU WILL NEED: A helper, pencil and paper.

YOU ARE GOING TO: make 20 in different ways.
❏ Take turns with your helper to say a pair of numbers that add up to 20. You have to give a **different** pair of numbers each time.
❏ Write them down as you say them.
❏ Keep on going until you can't think of any more.

❏ Take your pairs of numbers back to school.

HANDY HINT!
Use the pairs that make 10 to help you find pairs that make 20.

8

13 No, hang on, that's wrong. Let's check it.

BET YOU CAN'T
❏ Find all the pairs of numbers that add up to 21.

DEAR HELPER

THE POINT OF THIS ACTIVITY: is to help your child recognize the number pairs which add up to 20. Knowing these pairs will help when he or she is calculating with larger numbers.

YOU MIGHT LIKE TO:
● Ask your child how he or she can use the pairs that make 20 to make pairs for 22 (for example, 15 + 5 makes 20, so 15 + 7 makes 22).

● Go on to find pairs for 22, or let your child choose a target number.

IF YOU GET STUCK: try finding pairs which make 10. Then go on to make 20, using 20 objects. Your child can divide the objects between two groups to give a pair of numbers.

Please sign: . . . .

ADDITION AND SUBTRACTION

IMPACT

NAME   DATE

CROSS IT OUT

YOU WILL NEED: A helper, this game sheet, a dice, pencil and paper.

YOU ARE GOING TO: play an addition game.
❑ Decide who will start.
❑ If it is your turn to start, choose a number from the balloon. Then roll a dice and add the number rolled to your balloon number.
❑ If the answer is on your grid, cross it out.
❑ Now it is your helper's turn. The first player to cross out two rows of numbers on his or her grid is the winner.

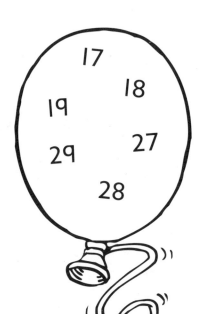

Player 1   Player 2

YOU MIGHT LIKE TO TRY
Playing on to see who can be the first to cross out all his or her numbers.

17 18 19 20 21 22 23 24 25 26 27 28 29 30 31 32 33 34 35

DEAR HELPER

THE POINT OF THIS ACTIVITY: is to help your child add a single-digit number to a 2-digit number mentally. It offers particularly good practice in 'bridging' across a ten (for example, adding 8 to 18 means that you have to 'bridge' across 20).

Encourage your child to add on a number which will bridge across a ten by adding up to the tens number, then adding on the rest. For example, 28 + 5 can be written as 28 + 2 + 3. You can add the 2 to 28 to make 30, then add the 3 to make 33. To use this method, you need to know the pairs of numbers that make 10.

YOU MIGHT LIKE TO: ask your child, when he or she has chosen a balloon number, what dice scores he or she needs to get in order to complete a row.

IF YOU GET STUCK:
• Use the number line above to help your child add by counting on.
• Practise the pairs of numbers that make 10.

Please sign: . . . .

NAME   **DATE**

MAKE IT

YOU WILL NEED: A helper, pencil and paper.

YOU ARE GOING TO: make some number sentences that involve addition and subtraction.

❏ Look at the numbers and symbols in the box below. You will use these to make number sentences.

```
12   8   7   +
2   15   1   −
10  13   3   =
```

❏ Choose **three** of the numbers to make an addition or subtraction sentence. Write it down. For example: 12 − 2 = 10.
❏ Ask your helper to write down a different addition or subtraction sentence, using only numbers and symbols from the box.
❏ Keep on taking turns until you can't make any more additions or subtractions.

❏ Take all the number sentences you've written down into school.

BET YOU CAN'T

Add 3 to each number in the box, then write down a new list of number sentences using the new numbers.

DEAR HELPER

THE POINT OF THIS ACTIVITY: is to help your child see connections between numbers and understand the relationship between addition and subtraction.
  Ask your child to read out the number sentences he or she has written. Encourage him or her to write down both additions and subtractions.

YOU MIGHT LIKE TO: ask your child whether the addition sentences might help him or her to write subtraction sentences, or vice versa. For example, if 17 + 4 = 21, then 21 − 4 = 17. Does it help him or her to find other related subtraction sentences (such as 21 − 17 = 4)? Seeing these patterns will help your child with calculation.

IF YOU GET STUCK: ask your child to suggest two of the numbers and look to see whether it makes one of the other numbers in the box.

Please sign: . . . .

CHAIN REACTION

YOU WILL NEED: A helper, pencil and paper.

YOU ARE GOING TO: solve an addition and subtraction puzzle.
❑ Fill in the missing numbers in the circles to make a complete number chain.

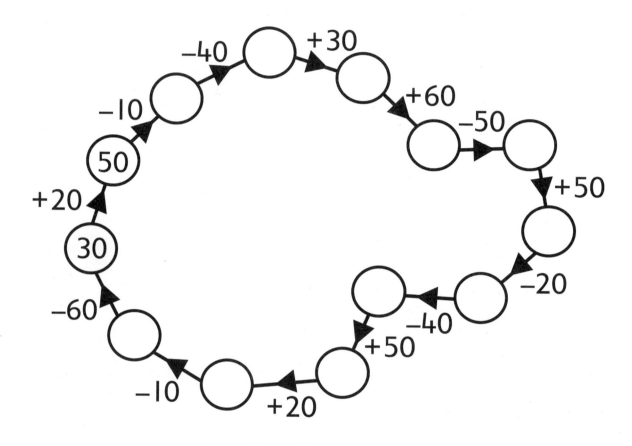

❑ Bring your completed chain back to school.

YOU MIGHT LIKE TO TRY
❑ Making up your own chain puzzle for your helper to fill in.

DEAR HELPER

THE POINT OF THIS ACTIVITY: is to help your child add and subtract mentally. Discuss with your child how he or she is adding and subtracting the numbers. Try to discourage him or her from counting on or back in ones.

YOU MIGHT LIKE TO: try making the first number 150 instead of 30, then going through the loop again. It is useful for your child to experience working with large numbers.

IF YOU GET STUCK: talk with your child about how he or she might add on or subtract these numbers by adding or subtracting 10 at a time.

Please sign: . . . .

NAME _____   DATE _____

A NUMBER CLOUD

YOU WILL NEED: A helper, pencil and paper.

YOU ARE GOING TO: add numbers in your head.
❑ Choose any number in the cloud. Now choose any other number in the cloud and add the two together. Try to work out the answer in your head.
❑ See how many different additions you can make.

❑ Bring all your additions into school.

0	1	2	3	4	5	6	7	8	9
10	11	12	13	14	15	16	17	18	19
20	21	22	23	24	25	26	27	28	29
30	31	32	33	34	35	36	37	38	39
40	41	42	43	44	45	46	47	48	49

BET YOU CAN'T
Find different pairs of numbers in the cloud that add together to give the same answer, and explain to your helper why they do that.

DEAR HELPER

THE POINT OF THIS ACTIVITY: is to give your child practice in adding two numbers mentally. Encourage your child to talk about what he or she is doing in his or her head. Starting with the larger of the two numbers each time can be helpful.

You could take turns to add a pair of numbers and explain how the addition was worked out. Although this is a mental activity, jotting down stages in the process can be helpful. For example: 22 + 13 is 22 + 10 + 3, that's 32 + 3 which is 35.

YOU MIGHT LIKE TO: Ask your child to find pairs of numbers in the grid above that add together to give the same answer. Can he or she find a pattern in these pairs of numbers?

IF YOU GET STUCK:
● Use the number grid above to help your child get started. Discourage him or her from adding on one unit at a time. Use the fact that going down is counting on in tens and going across is counting on in units. So 24 + 13 is 24, down 10, across 3 to 37.

Please sign: _____

SUBTRACTION SAM

YOU WILL NEED: A helper, pencil and paper.

YOU ARE GOING TO: subtract small numbers from numbers over 30.

❑ With your helper, look at Subtraction Sam. Talk about what you think he is doing.

❑ Fill in the OUT boxes to show the answers to Sam's subtractions.

❑ Put a number in the first empty IN box. Your helper has to put the right number in the OUT box. Swap over and repeat, then swap back for the last one.

❑ Bring Sam back to school with all the boxes filled in.

YOU MIGHT LIKE TO TRY

❑ Drawing another subtraction machine. You can name it and decide what it is going to subtract. Show some numbers (bigger than 30) going into the machine, and write answers in the OUT boxes.

❑ Drawing another subtraction machine, with IN numbers bigger than 100.

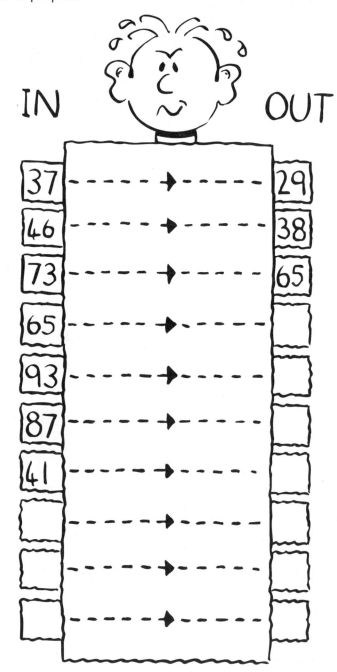

DEAR HELPER

THE POINT OF THIS ACTIVITY: is to help your child subtract single-digit numbers from 2-digit numbers. Encourage your child to read the numbers and then work out the answers mentally.

YOU MIGHT LIKE TO:
• Try different subtraction numbers.
• Try some new, larger IN numbers.

IF YOU GET STUCK: encourage your child to count on from each OUT number to the IN number in order to find the difference. Check that it's the same each time. Then your child can count back from each IN number to find the OUT number.

Please sign: . . . .

CALENDAR TIME

YOU WILL NEED: A helper, a calendar (unless you already know how many days are in each month), paper and pencil.

YOU ARE GOING TO: add together numbers that are close to 30.
❑ Write down a list of the months of the year and how many days are in each. Use a calendar to help you if necessary.

❑ In your head, work out how many days there are altogether in January and February. Write down the answer.
❑ Now try February + March, then March + April and so on. Carry on until you have done November + December.
❑ How many different additions have you done?
❑ Bring your list of additions to school.

BET YOU CAN'T
❑ Add three months at a time in your head.

DEAR HELPER

THE POINT OF THIS ACTIVITY: is to encourage mental addition. It will also help your child to learn the months and the number of days in each month.
   Encourage your child to say the months in order and to find out how many days there are in each one. Talk about how the two numbers can be added mentally. Encourage your child to use facts that he or she already knows. For example: 'If 30 + 30 is 60, then 31 + 30 is 61'.

YOU MIGHT LIKE TO: talk about leap years. What would January + February and February + March be in a leap year?

IF YOU GET STUCK: talk with your child about adding on 10 at a time, for example starting with 31 and counting on in tens.

Please sign: . . . .

| NAME | DATE |

TAKE IT UP

YOU WILL NEED: A helper, pencil and paper.

YOU ARE GOING TO: find numbers which add to make 20.
- Play this game with your helper. One player says a number between 10 and 20, and the other player has to say the number needed to make a total of 20 with the first number. Write down the addition.
- Take turns until you think you have found all the ways of making 20.
- Make sure you have written down all the additions. Bring them back to school.

BET YOU CAN'T
- Use starting numbers between 20 and 30 and make a total of 30 each time.

DEAR HELPER

THE POINT OF THIS ACTIVITY: is to offer your child practice in adding on to make the next ten – in this case, adding on to make 20 from numbers over 10. In time, your child will 'just know' what number needs to be added.

Encourage your child to say the addition. This will help him or her to remember it. For example, if you have said 16, your child might say: '16 and 4 equals 20'.

YOU MIGHT LIKE TO: try other versions, such as making 40 from numbers over 30. For a greater challenge, ask your child to take the number to the 'next but one' ten: from 13 to 30, rather than 20.

IF YOU GET STUCK: use a ruler or make a simple number line, so that your child can find the starting number and then count on from it.

Please sign: . . . .

ADDITION AND SUBTRACTION

IMPACT

NAME	DATE

TOP SCORER

YOU WILL NEED: A helper, pencil and paper, the 'Goal scorers' sheet (page 26).

YOU ARE GOING TO: add up numbers of goals!
Droitwich Football Club's star striker, Darren Wain, has scored 43 goals in this season. The picture below shows how many times he has scored in each part of the goal.

❏ Which **two** of the numbers in the goal add up to make each of these totals?
   11   15   12   10   16   19   17

❏ Which **three** of the numbers in the goal add up to make each of these totals?
   15   21   23   25   27

❏ Bring this sheet, and the 'Goal scorers' sheet if you have filled it in, back to school.

BET YOU CAN'T

❏ See which totals you can make using any **four** or **five** of the numbers shown in the goal.

❏ Fill in the 'Goal scorers' sheet to show 19 goals scored by each player.

DEAR HELPER

THE POINT OF THIS ACTIVITY: is to help with mental addition of more than two numbers. It also requires your child to consider problems that have more than one correct answer.

Start by talking about the picture. Ask your child to check that the total number of goals shown is 43.

YOU MIGHT LIKE TO: encourage your child to derive new totals using slightly different combinations from those he or she has already found.

IF YOU GET STUCK: See what different totals you can make using only two of the numbers in the goal. Count with your child to reach these totals.

Please sign: . . . .

GOAL SCORERS

These goals show where different players have scored. 19 goals were scored by each player.

❑ Can you fill in the blanks to show that each player has scored **19 goals**?

Make 19 goals in total

Make 19 goals

Make 19 goals

Make 19 goals

Make 19 goals

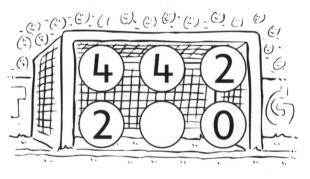

Make 19 goals

MAKING MESSY NUMBERS

YOU WILL NEED: A helper, pencil and paper.

YOU ARE GOING TO: solve a problem by adding and subtracting.
❏ To solve this problem, you are only allowed to **add** or **subtract**.

You have to make 27 using eight different numbers, but you are not allowed to use 1 or 2.

❏ Write down **five** different ways of making 27. You must stick to the rules given above!

❏ Now try making 10 using **six** different numbers, but not using 1 or 2. Here is one possible way:

3 + 7 + 9 + 11 – 8 – 12 = 10

❏ Bring all your answers, and any problems you have made up, back to school.

YOU MIGHT LIKE TO TRY
❏ Making up a problem of your own, using a different target number and deciding how many numbers can be used. Then see whether your helper can solve it!

DEAR HELPER

THE POINT OF THIS ACTIVITY: is to help your child add up several numbers mentally, and develop mental strategies for solving problems. 'Messy' numbers are numbers which are not multiples of 5 or 10, and so tend to lead to difficult maths questions! Encourage your child to write down all his or her attempts, not just the successful ones.

YOU MIGHT LIKE TO: extend this by posing similar problems, such as 'Can you make 17 using any eight different numbers?'

IF YOU GET STUCK:
● Try making any number below 10, using only three different numbers.
● Try letting your child use numbers more than once.

Please sign: . . . .

NAME   DATE

UP AND DOWN DICE

YOU WILL NEED: A helper, a dice, pencil and paper.

YOU ARE GOING TO: play an adding and subtracting game.

I've hit the target! My start number was 120 and my target was 180. I threw a 3 and added 30 to make 150. Then I threw a 6 and added 60 to make 210. Then I threw a 3 and subtracted 30 to make 180!

❏ Choose any multiple of 10 between 100 and 200 (such as 110, 130 or 180) to be your **start number**, and another one to be your **target number**. Write them both down.

❏ Take turns with your helper to roll the dice. Multiply the number you roll by 10. This is your **dice number**.

❏ Starting with your start number, you can add **or** subtract the dice number to get nearer to your target number.

❏ Keep a note of your scores as you play. If you hit your target, you win. After ten throws each, if neither player has hit the target, the player who is closest wins.

❏ Play the game ten times, with a different start and target number each time. Record how often you hit your target, and how many throws it takes each time.

❏ Bring your results back to school.

BET YOU CAN'T

❏ Choose numbers between 400 and 500 for your start number and target number.

DEAR HELPER

THE POINT OF THIS ACTIVITY: is to give your child practice in addition and subtraction of 10s, and to encourage your child to record his or her results in a systematic way.

YOU MIGHT LIKE TO:
● Ask your child to think about how often he or she is able to get to the target in 10 goes. Are some targets easier to reach than others?

● Set the start and target numbers at a higher level, such as 600–700. It is good for your child to practise using big numbers.

IF YOU GET STUCK:
● Count in 10s with your child.
● Try only throwing the dice five times before you stop.

Please sign: ....

TELEPHONE KEYPAD

YOU WILL NEED: A helper, pencil and paper.

YOU ARE GOING TO: choose numbers to make different totals. Here is a telephone keypad:

❏ Choose any four numbers and add them together. Write down the numbers and the total.
❏ Choose another four numbers and do the same thing.
❏ Can you find four numbers to make each of the following totals?

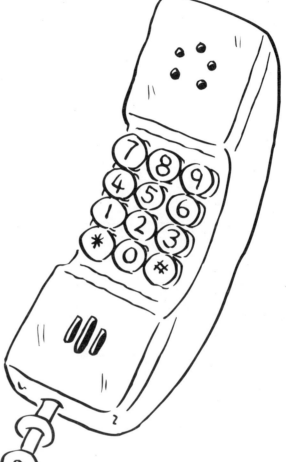

```
10   20   30
 9   19   29
 8   18   28
 7   17   27
```

❏ Bring your paper with the numbers written on it back to school.

YOU MIGHT LIKE TO TRY
Making all the numbers up to 30 by adding four of the keyboard numbers. Are there any numbers that you cannot make?

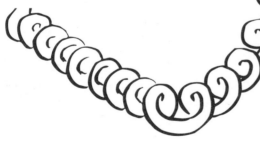

DEAR HELPER

THE POINT OF THIS ACTIVITY: is to help your child with multiple additions (such as 3 + 4 + 5 + 6). It will also let your child work on an open-ended problem (that is, a problem with more than one correct answer).

YOU MIGHT LIKE TO:
● Ask your child to find the smallest total and the largest total possible using four numbers.

● Ask your child: *What totals are not possible if you cannot use the 6 key?*

IF YOU GET STUCK: Start by adding only two or three numbers together, then writing down the numbers and the total.

Please sign: . . . .

CALCULATOR KEYPAD

YOU WILL NEED: A helper, pencil and paper, the 'More keypads' sheet (page 31).

YOU ARE GOING TO: practise adding three numbers together in your head.

❑ Look at this calculator keypad.
❑ Choose any row and any column of numbers.
❑ Add up all the numbers in the row and the column. For example:

the first column   7 + 4 + 1 = 12
the second row   4 + 5 + 6 = 15
TOTAL   27

❑ Make a list of other numbers that you can make in this way.
❑ Bring your list of numbers back to school.

YOU MIGHT LIKE TO TRY

❑ Looking at the other keypads on page 31. What numbers can you make by adding up the diagonals in them?

DEAR HELPER

THE POINT OF THIS ACTIVITY: is to help your child with multiple additions (such as 3 + 4 + 5 + 6). It will also give your child an opportunity to work systematically on an investigation over a sustained period of time, finding all the possible answers.

YOU MIGHT LIKE TO: ask your child to try the same investigation with any other keypads you have in the home (such as a telephone keypad).

IF YOU GET STUCK: start by adding only two or three numbers, writing down the numbers and the total.

Please sign: . . . .

MORE KEYPADS

Here are some different types of keypads.
❑ Use them to add diagonal lines of numbers. What numbers can you make?

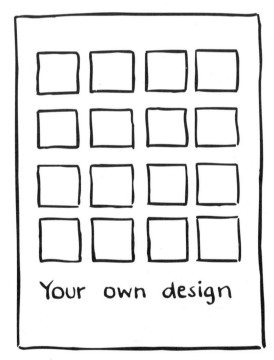

NAME   DATE

CROSS AND COUNT

YOU WILL NEED: a helper, pencil and paper.

YOU ARE GOING TO: choose numbers and add them in your head to make a target number.
❑ Look at the first grid below. You will see 16 numbers.
❑ You and your helper take it in turns to cross out a number. Add up the numbers you cross out as you go.
❑ Can you and your helper work together to cross out a total of 27?

❑ Now use the second grid to try crossing out a total of 36.
❑ Bring your grids back into school.

5	4	3	2
1	5	7	9
9	7	5	4
9	9	3	8

5	4	3	2
1	5	7	9
9	7	5	4
9	9	3	8

BET YOU CAN'T
Have a starting number of 25 and add numbers from the grid (draw circles around them) to get to 57.

DEAR HELPER

THE POINT OF THIS ACTIVITY: is to help your child develop a method for calculating what number is needed to make the target number. This involves both addition of the numbers crossed out and subtraction from the target number. Deciding which grid number to cross out next requires your child to think ahead.

YOU MIGHT LIKE TO:
● Set a different target number or starting number.

● Set a small target number and add or subtract a grid number each time.
● Start with a different grid (perhaps a 5 × 5 grid).

IF YOU GET STUCK: Make a simple number line (or use a ruler) to help your child count on or back.

Please sign: . . . .

NAME   DATE

HALVE AND HALVE AGAIN

YOU WILL NEED: A helper, pencil and paper.

YOU ARE GOING TO: find halves and quarters of numbers.

❏ Look at Henry Halve-and-Halve-Again. As you can see, he's made a bit of a mess. Can you and your helper sort it out?

❏ You will need to check the answers Henry has given. He was supposed to halve a number, then halve it again, like this:

IN   halve   halve again   OUT

`[24]` — — — — — — — — — `[6]`

❏ But as you can see, he has got some of them wrong. Check his answers and write down the correct ones where necessary.

❏ Bring your list of correct answers back to school.

BET YOU CAN'T

Halve and halve again the number of minutes in an hour.

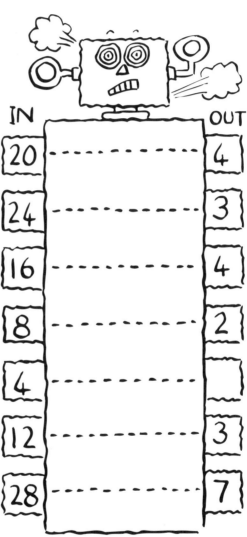

DEAR HELPER

THE POINT OF THIS ACTIVITY: is to help your child halve numbers mentally and use this to find quarters of numbers which divide by 4. Encourage your child to decide which answers are wrong and tell you why.

YOU MIGHT LIKE TO: give Henry more numbers. They should all be from the 4 times table – for example, 32, 44, 48, or more difficult ones such as 68, 96 or 120.

IF YOU GET STUCK: use some objects, such as buttons, bits of paper or pegs, so that your child can physically find half of each number, then halve it again. Encourage your child to say what each half is: 'I've found half of 12, it's 6. Then half of 6 is 3.'

Please sign: . . . .

LINE UP

YOU WILL NEED: A helper, a pack of cards, the playing grid below, a different coloured pencil each.

YOU ARE GOING TO: practise multiplying numbers by 5.

❑ Take the Jacks, Queens and Kings out of the pack. Shuffle the cards that are left and place them face down in a pile.
❑ Turn over the top card and multiply this number by 5. Find the answer on the grid and cross it off with your coloured pencil.
❑ Now it is your helper's turn to do the same thing.
❑ The first player to cross out four numbers in a line with his or her colour is the winner! The line can be across, down or diagonal.
❑ Bring the grid back to school. Be ready to explain how the numbers were crossed out.

BET YOU CAN'T
Work out which cards the loser would have needed to win.

35	50	50	35	40	15
25	45	5	40	20	15
45	50	30	10	10	15
5	15	45	30	20	25
10	5	10	40	20	35
5	30	35	30	25	20

DEAR HELPER

THE POINT OF THIS ACTIVITY: is to give your child practice in multiplying by 5. Encourage your child to say the number on the card, as well as the answer when multiplied by 5.
  If you don't have playing cards, you could use small pieces of paper with the numbers 1 to 10 written on.

YOU MIGHT LIKE TO:
● Ask your child, halfway through the game, what cards he or she needs to turn over in order to win.

● Play a pairs game. Spread the cards out face down and take turns to choose two cards. If the two cards add to make a number that, multiplied by 5, makes 50, you keep the cards. See which of you wins more cards.

IF YOU GET STUCK: you and your child could count together in fives, perhaps using your fingers to help (see illustration).

Please sign: . . . .

| NAME | DATE |

DOG FOOD

YOU WILL NEED: A helper, some different coloured crayons (with light colours).

YOU ARE GOING TO: recognize numbers in the 3, 4 and 5 times tables.
The three dogs below can only chew bones with numbers that are in their own times tables.

❏ Colour each dog and its bones with the same crayon. Some of the bones will be chewed by more than one dog!
❏ Each dog likes to chew 7 bones a day. Do they all have enough bones?
❏ Bring your 'dogs and bones' picture back to school.

BET YOU CAN'T
Draw some more bones with numbers, then colour them in.

DEAR HELPER

THE POINT OF THIS ACTIVITY: is to help your child learn the multiples of 3, 4 and 5 – that is, the numbers in the 3, 4 and 5 times tables. He or she will need to know these numbers in order to complete the activity.

Encourage your child to check carefully when deciding how to colour in each bone, and when counting the bones that will be chewed by each dog. You might suggest that your child draw a line from the dog to each of its bones. A useful strategy is to look at all the bones for one hungry dog (that is, one multiplication table) at a time.

YOU MIGHT LIKE TO: ask your child to draw all the bones for the dogs (that is, all the numbers in the 3, 4 and 5 times tables). Then ask your child to close his or her eyes. Cover up a bone, then ask your child to look. Tell him or her which dog(s) will have one bone less. Ask: *Which bone is missing?*

IF YOU GET STUCK: start with the 5 dot and ask your child what the numbers in the bones will end with.

Please sign: . . . .

PICKLES THE GREEDY CAT

YOU WILL NEED: A helper, pencil and paper.

YOU ARE GOING TO: practise dividing numbers by 4.

Pickles loves to eat crunchy 'kitty treats'. He eats them 4 at a time. Here are some of his dinner bowls. The number of treats in each bowl is written on the side.

❑ Which bowls can he eat from 4 treats at a time and not have any treats left over? Put a tick on the mat under each of these bowls.

❑ For the other bowls, write on the mat how many treats are left over. The first one has been done for you.

❑ Bring this page back to school.

BET YOU CAN'T

❑ Draw some more bowls with numbers on, then work out whether Pickles will have any treats left over in each bowl.

DEAR HELPER

THE POINT OF THIS ACTIVITY: is to help your child remember the multiples of 4, learn which numbers divide by 4 exactly, and understand the idea of remainders.

YOU MIGHT LIKE TO: vary the activity by saying that Pickles eats the 'kitty treats' 5 or 6 at a time.

IF YOU GET STUCK: go through the 4 times table together. Tell your child not to worry about writing the remainders; or provide numbers that are all exact multiples of 4.

Please sign: . . . .

BECKY'S BUGS

YOU WILL NEED: A helper, pencil and paper.

YOU ARE GOING TO: look at the 3 times table.
Becky collects bugs. She has collected six so far.

❑ Look at the first bug. Six multiples of 3 have been written on its legs, in order. The last number has also been written on its body. Say these numbers out loud.
❑ Some of the bugs have a multiple of 3 written on the first leg. Write the next five multiples of 3 on the other legs – so if the first leg is 15, carry on with 18, 21 and so on. Write the last number on the body as well.
❑ Some of the bugs have the final number already written on the body. With these bugs, you have to count back in steps of 3 to find the start number on the first leg.
❑ Bring all your completed bugs back to school.

BET YOU CAN'T
❑ Draw another set of bugs and write multiples of 4 on each bug's legs.

DEAR HELPER

THE POINT OF THIS ACTIVITY: is to help your child learn the 3 times table by writing and saying the multiples of 3 in order. Work through an example of each type of bug with your child to show him or her how to find and write down the answers.

YOU MIGHT LIKE TO: vary the activity by using a different multiplication table (any table up to 10 × 10).

IF YOU GET STUCK: try counting in 2s first, to practise the 2 times table, then count aloud in 3s.

Please sign: . . . .

NAME   DATE

FOUR THROWS

YOU WILL NEED: A helper, two dice, pencil and paper.

YOU ARE GOING TO: Look for multiples of 4.
- Roll both dice. Use the two numbers to make a 2-digit number. For example, if you get a 3 and a 6, you could make 36 or 63. Write down each number you make and whether it is a multiple of 4.
- You can have four throws of the dice, trying each time to make a multiple of 4. How many times do you succeed?
- Now your helper has four throws of the dice. Who made more multiples of 4?
- Play the game again. Who wins this time?
- Bring the paper with your numbers on back to school.

YOU MIGHT LIKE TO TRY
Adding extra rules, such as: *Make the 2-digit number and then add or subtract one of the numbers to make a multiple of 4.* For example, if you throw a 3 and a 5, you can make 35, then take away 3 to make 32.

DEAR HELPER

THE POINT OF THIS ACTIVITY: is to help your child practise the 4 times table. Your child needs to be familiar with the multiples of 4 to decide what numbers to make with the dice.

YOU MIGHT LIKE TO: ask your child to make a multiple of 3 in three throws, or one of 5 in five throws.

IF YOU GET STUCK: ask your child to write down the multiples of 4 (up to 64) in a list before rolling the dice.

Please sign: . . . .

NAME   DATE

DIVIDE AND RULE

YOU WILL NEED: A helper, this sheet, the 'More tracks' sheet (page 40), a dice, two different counters (or coins), pencil and paper.

YOU ARE GOING TO: play a division game.
- You and your helper each put a counter at START on the track.
- Take turns to roll the dice. If the number you roll goes **exactly** into the next number on the track, you may move on to that number. If it doesn't, you stay where you are!
- Each time you can move, write down **how many times** your number goes into the number on the path.
- When you reach 21, you can go straight on to FINISH – and win!
- Bring what you have written back to school.

YOU MIGHT LIKE TO TRY
The two other tracks on page 40 – or fill in the blank one to make your own.

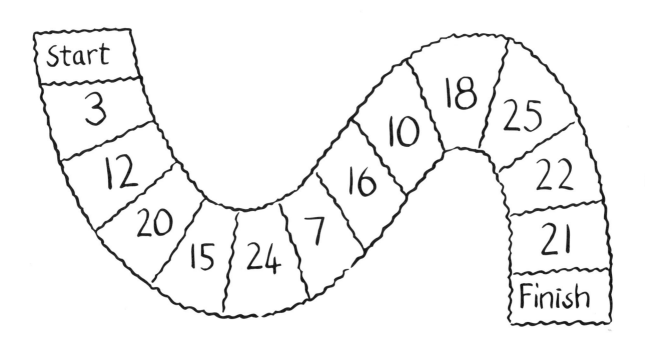

DEAR HELPER

THE POINT OF THIS ACTIVITY: is to help your child with mental multiplication and division. Encourage your child to say, each time he or she moves forward, how many times the dice number goes into the track number. For example: '4 goes into 24 six times exactly'.

YOU MIGHT LIKE TO:
- Ask your child each time what dice score he or she needs to move to the next space.

- Ask your child what the remainder is when the track number is not a multiple of the dice number.

IF YOU GET STUCK: Count with your child the times table of the number shown on the dice, to see whether your child can move forward to the next space.

Please sign: . . . .

MORE TRACKS

Here are two more number tracks – and one that has been left blank.

❑ Each section of this track shows a number from 1 to 36. In the rest of the space, write how many times the number on your dice goes into it. The first two have been done for you.

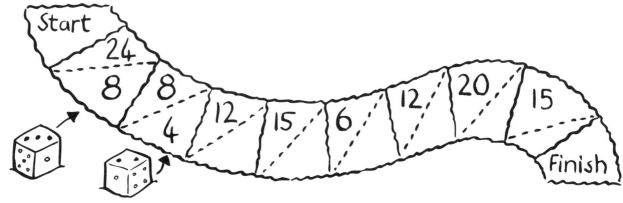

❑ Write your own numbers on this blank track, then use it to play the same game.

❑ Now play on this special track. If you don't get the numbers where the rats live in one or two throws, you have to escape by going back through the tunnels!

MENTAL MATHS HOMEWORK

NAME   DATE

WINNING GOAL

YOU WILL NEED: A helper, two dice, pencil and paper.

YOU ARE GOING TO: play another football maths game!
- You and your helper each choose a number from 2 to 5 as your 'goal' number.
- Decide which player will start.

- If you are starting, roll both dice and multiply the two numbers. If the number you get (the **product** of the two dice numbers) is an exact multiple of your goal number, you score a goal. If not, you have missed.

  For example, if your goal number is 2 and you throw 3 and 4, your score is 3 × 4 = 12. This is a multiple of 2, so you have scored.
- Now your helper tries to score.
- After five turns each, the player with more goals is the winner.
- Bring your game results back to school.

BET YOU CAN'T
Work out which is the best number to choose as a goal number.

DEAR HELPER

THE POINT OF THIS ACTIVITY: is to practise mental multiplication and division. In order to score a 'goal', your child has to multiply the two dice numbers and then divide the product by his or her 'goal' number.

YOU MIGHT LIKE TO: choose a particular 'goal number' for both players to use (perhaps 3). Discuss with your child why he or she cannot choose 1 as the 'goal' number (because then every number would 'score', and the game would be pointless).

IF YOU GET STUCK: try adding the dice numbers instead of multiplying them, and 'scoring' if the total is an even number.

Please sign: . . . .

MONSTER DIGITS

YOU WILL NEED: A helper, some pencils, paper.

YOU ARE GOING TO: use art to help you think about multiples of 3.

❏ Draw a monster that has three heads and three arms, with three hands on each arm and three fingers on each hand.

❏ How many fingers would three of these monsters have between them? Write down the answer and show how you worked it out.

❏ Bring your monster picture and calculations back to school.

BET YOU CAN'T

❏ Draw a 'four' monster with four heads, arms, hands and fingers.

❏ Work out how many fingers four of these monsters would have between them.

DEAR HELPER

THE POINT OF THIS ACTIVITY: is to help your child practise working with multiples of 3. To solve the problem, your child will need to work systematically and explain his or her thinking.

YOU MIGHT LIKE TO: ask your child to draw other monsters with other numerical attributes. Then ask your child questions about them, such as 'How many legs do these three monsters have between them?'

IF YOU GET STUCK: try counting the fingers on one monster, then extending it to two, then three.

Please sign: . . . .

ROLL AND ROLL AGAIN

YOU WILL NEED: A helper, a dice, pencil and paper.

YOU ARE GOING TO: play a multiplying and subtracting game.
❑ Let your helper go first. He or she must roll the dice, say the number, then multiply it by 10 and tell you the answer. Write this number down.
❑ Now your helper rolls the dice again, multiplies by 10 and tells you the answer. You write it down.
❑ Your helper now has to find the difference between these two numbers and tell you. If your helper has got it right, and you agree, then it is your turn to roll the dice.
❑ Take turns to play. Tell each other exactly what you are doing. Keep on playing until you have had ten goes each.

❑ Bring your work into school.

BET YOU CAN'T
Multiply the dice numbers by 100 and find the difference.

0 10 20 30 40 50 60 70 80 90 100

DEAR HELPER

THE POINT OF THIS ACTIVITY: is to help your child multiply numbers by 10 and subtract one multiple of 10 from another.

It may be helpful to encourage your child to count on out loud when finding the difference. As you go first, you could demonstrate this way of finding the difference on your first turn. However, your child may 'just know' some of the differences without having to work them out.

YOU MIGHT LIKE TO: use the cards Ace to 10. Shuffle them and turn over two at a time, then multiply by 10 and find the difference.

IF YOU GET STUCK: join in with your child in counting on to the higher number. You could use the number line above to help with this.

Please sign: . . . .

TARGET 75

YOU WILL NEED: A helper, a dice, pencil and paper.

YOU ARE GOING TO: Play an adding, subtracting and multiplying game.
- ❏ Choose a **start number** from 1 to 10. Your **target number** is 75.
- ❏ Roll the dice and write down the number. You can choose whether to add this number to, subtract it from or multiply it by your start number to make a new running total.
- ❏ Roll the dice again and repeat, until your running total is exactly 75.

For example, if you choose 4 as your start number, then roll a 3, you could choose to multiply $4 \times 3 = 12$.

If you then roll 2, you could choose to multiply $12 \times 2 = 24$.

If you then roll 6, you could choose to add $6 + 24 = 30$... and so on until you reach 75.

- ❏ Count how many times you had to roll the dice to reach 75.
- ❏ Now it is your helper's turn to do the same thing. Can he or she reach 75 with fewer throws of the dice than you?

- ❏ Bring your results back to school.

YOU MIGHT LIKE TO TRY
- ❏ Playing again with a different start number or target number.

DEAR HELPER

THE POINT OF THIS ACTIVITY: is to let your child try a mixed-operation activity – in this case, using addition, subtraction and multiplication. It also requires strategic thinking to select the best operation each time (for example, using multiplication to make the number get bigger quickly). Try to encourage your child to use multiplication in this way.

Encourage your child to write down his or her choices, and to keep a running total. This will help him or her to develop good recording skills, as well as providing a record of the game to take back to school.

YOU MIGHT LIKE TO: use a set of cards (Ace to 10) instead of a dice, turning over one card at a time.

IF YOU GET STUCK: try the activity without a target number, just trying to reach as high a total as possible in five throws.

Please sign: . . . .

NAME _____   DATE _____

GOING UNDERGROUND

YOU WILL NEED: A helper, pencil and paper.

YOU ARE GOING TO: practise adding and multiplying.

Matt the mole likes to store his food deep underground. Each tunnel ends in a store of food.

❑ Choose a number between 0 and 11.
❑ Start at the entrance and follow Matt down to the first store of food. You must change the number as it says in each tunnel.
❑ When you get to the end, write the answer above the food store.
❑ Go back to the entrance and go to the next food store, and so on until you have visited all the food stores.

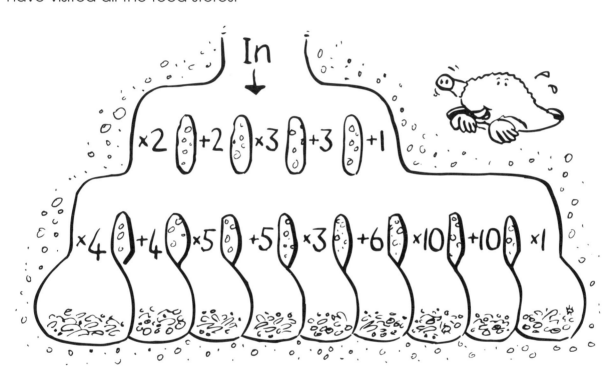

❑ Bring your tunnel picture, showing which way the mole went, back to school.

BET YOU CAN'T
Find the largest and the smallest possible food store number.

DEAR HELPER

THE POINT OF THIS ACTIVITY: is to introduce your child to a **flow chart** in which different instructions follow in sequence. This particular flow chart helps your child to practise multi-step operations which include addition and multiplication.

YOU MIGHT LIKE TO: give your child some finish numbers and ask him or her to work backwards through the tunnels. This is much more difficult.

IF YOU GET STUCK:
● Stick to start numbers between 0 and 5.
● Simplify the tunnel instructions by using smaller numbers (but keep the mixture of operations).

Please sign: . . . .

NAME   DATE

PRINTING PROBLEMS

YOU WILL NEED: A helper, pencil and paper.

YOU ARE GOING TO: solve a problem by thinking logically.

This book has 100 pages. They should be numbered 1–100, but at the printer's the number 7 did not print correctly: it came out as 1.

❏ How many pages will be printed with the wrong number?

❏ Make a list of all the pages with wrong numbers.

❏ Bring your answer and list back to school.

BET YOU CAN'T

❏ Work out how many pages would be numbered wrongly if the book had 1000 pages.

DEAR HELPER

THE POINT OF THIS ACTIVITY: is to help your child work through a numerical problem logically, recording his or her work in a systematic way. He or she will need have a knowledge of units, tens and hundreds.

YOU MIGHT LIKE TO: suggest other wrong digits. Is there always the same number of wrongly numbered pages when one digit is wrong, whichever digit it is?

IF YOU GET STUCK: try using a book of 20 pages and a misprinted number 5. Build up the complexity of the problem from this.

Please sign: . . . .

NAME _____ DATE _____

CHAIN LINKS

YOU WILL NEED: a helper, pencil and paper.

YOU ARE GOING TO: make some number chains by adding, subtracting and multiplying.

❑ Look at the four chains below. Each chain has some empty spaces and some numbers. The links tell you what to do to make the next number – for example, +7 or ×2.

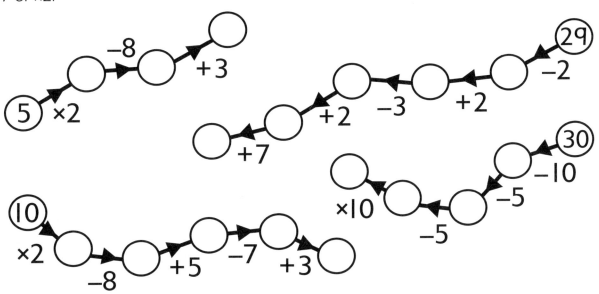

❑ Look at the chain which starts with 5. Can you work out the rest of the chain? Write the numbers in the spaces as you go along.
❑ Now complete the other three chains.

❑ Bring your chains back to school.

YOU MIGHT LIKE TO TRY
❑ Making up your own chain, using the blank chain below. You must finish it!

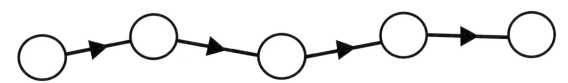

DEAR HELPER

THE POINT OF THIS ACTIVITY: is to help your child with addition, subtraction and multiplication operations, and to give him or her a multi-step challenge including all of these. Sometimes your child will have to work backwards, which involves using the **inverse** (or opposite) operation: using subtraction as the inverse of addition (and vice versa), and division as the inverse of multiplication.

YOU MIGHT LIKE TO: provide both ends of a chain – your child has to work out what to put in the middle.

IF YOU GET STUCK: make a simple chain using only one operation (perhaps addition), with the first number provided.

Please sign: . . . .

Dear Parent

We all know that parents are a crucial factor in their children's learning. You can make a huge difference to your child's education. We are planning to send home some activities that fit in with the maths we are doing in school. The activities are designed for your child to do with you, or another available adult. You do not need to know a lot of maths in order to help your child.

These are not traditional homework activities. It is important that your child first explains the activity to you. Each activity will have been explained thoroughly in school. Then do the activity together. By sharing these activities with your child, you will be helping to develop her or his mental maths. And as a result of being given that all-important attention, your child is more likely to become confident and skilled in maths.

We hope, too, that these activities will be fun to do – it matters that children develop positive attitudes to maths. If you are particularly nervous about maths, try not to make your child nervous too! If your child is having difficulties, look at the 'If you get stuck' suggestions which are provided on each activity sheet.

After completing each activity, your child will usually have something to bring back to school. However, sometimes there may not be anything written down to bring back – your child is doing mental maths, so all the work may be in your heads!

If you have any problems with or further questions about any of the activities – or about any of the maths being covered – please do let us know at school. We do very much value your support.

Yours sincerely